More th

Understanding and Growing in Your Relationship with Your Spiritual Father

Randy Borders

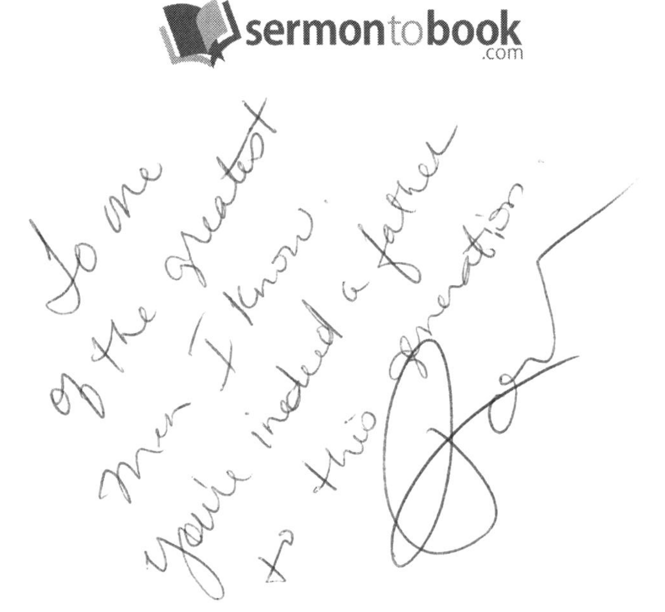

Sermon To Book
www.sermontobook.com

More than a Mentor / Randy Borders
ISBN-13: 978-1-945793-35-6
ISBN-10: 1-945793-35-X

There seems to be a tendency in many Christian contexts to abandon doctrines that have been abused. However, I would contend that you don't correct wrong teaching by non-teaching. You correct it by right teaching. I believe this is the heart of this book by Bishop Randy Borders. He takes an often-abandoned New Testament concept, spiritual parenting, and passionately and soundly highlights the importance of being raised to maturity in the faith. As Peter was to Mark, Elijah was to Elisha, and Paul was to Timothy, we need fathers in faith. My life and my leadership are better because of those who chose to be "more than a mentor."

Dr. Dharius Daniels
Lead Pastor, Change Church
Author, *RePresent Jesus*

Paul's words to the saints at Corinth that *"we have not many fathers,"* have never been more true than right now. In this millennial age where the Biblical concept of spiritual fathers is not necessarily a popular subject, we need clarity as to why this is the case and how to embrace this needed principle in the 21st century. With fresh insight and the pen of a ready writer, Bishop Randy Borders reveals the heart of God as a good Father and the valid priority for spiritual father-son relationships in the Kingdom of God. As a reverent son and amazing father in his own right, who better to peel back the layers of this matter and make the case for covering and spiritual authority being *more than a mentor*, than Randy Borders. Open your heart, ready your spirit and apply the practical wisdom from this long overdue treatise.

Bishop Kenneth Yelverton, D. Min.

Senior Pastor, The Temple of Refuge, Charlotte, NC

Author, *Sex and the Kingdom*

In an age when modern spiritual parenting often resembles a pyramid scheme, Bishop Randy Borders sounds a trumpet of clarity. This clarity concerning the spiritual parent-spiritual child relationship comes from the authentic experiences of one who has been both faithful son and loving father. Hence, Bishop Borders is legitimately qualified to offer such sage advice on this subject. We owe a debt of gratitude to God that this information is now accessible. The extraordinary wisdom in this book will undoubtedly help the Body of Christ recover the transformative power of this divine gift. Thank God for this work! Thank God for Bishop Randy Borders!

John R. Faison, Sr.

Senior Pastor, Watson Grove Missionary Baptist Church, Nashville, TN

Bishop Randy Borders is one of the greatest thinkers of his generation. God has illuminated him with wisdom on an array of Kingdom topics. He is a great husband, father, and pastor, but more apropos, he is a spiritual father to many. His insights are inspiring and his challenge firm so that the best of sons will get the most from their relationship with their spiritual fathers. I recommend this read as a staple in every spiritual father's library seeking to pour into their sons, and for every son seeking to maximize the time God has given you with their spiritual fathers. It is more than mentoring, indeed.

Bishop Terrell Fletcher

Senior Pastor, City of Hope International Church, San Diego, CA

Author, *The Book of You*

More than a Mentor by Bishop Borders is a recommended authentic product which reflects the personal journey he has willingly traveled. His humility is the "hidden in plain sight" backdrop for a bold description of the responsibilities to be placed squarely on the shoulders of both mentor and mentee. Consequently, this book serves most vividly as a comprehensive tool for the metaphorical drafting of a Memorandum of Understanding which reflects a practical theology and minimizes the risk of subsequent disagreements. I continue to applaud Bishop Borders' discontent with limiting his impact to the preaching realm as he leaves an instructional trail for subsequent generations. This work will be helpful as it weaves its way from pulpits, to classrooms, to nightstands, and ultimately to bearing the sign of frequently turned down corners as it occupies a permanent place on the practitioner's desk.

Dr. Cynthia Rembert James

The Potter's House, Dallas, TX

Author, *The Anointing*

Bishop Randy Borders has done it again. He is a man with dynamic preaching ability who is able to reveal the hidden pearls of the scripture. His gifting is even more than evident in his latest work, *More than a Mentor*. While many pastors feel unappreciated for all that they pour out, Bishop Borders takes tremendous care in lifting those who accept the call to be "more than a mentor." As always, his accurate prophetic anointing speaks exactly where people are, galvanizing them to their pastor's heart.

The words that Randy Borders speak are not contrived merely from reading and observing, God has raised him up as a father in the kingdom and graced him to serve churches and pastors across the length and breadth of this country. He has served our congregation time and time again. Each time he finishes ministering you can conclude that Bishop Borders is indeed a pastor's friend.

Clarence E. McClendon

Senior Pastor, The Place of Grace, Los Angeles, CA

Author, *Beyond Personal Power*

There is currently a dearth of real, sincere spiritual leadership in the world and church. We have unfortunately relegated the role that fathers should exist into mentors who we can shed at the first sign of disappointment or disagreement. Fathers take on the role of life leaders not just moment managers. Bishop Randy Borders has captured this sentiment and relayed it in easily digestible anecdotes and principles meant to build the body of Christ and the individual alike. Get a cup of your favorite beverage and allow *More than a Mentor* to help shape your understanding about spiritual (and natural) fatherhood.

Bishop Jason Nelson

Senior Pastor, The Tabernacle at Greater Bethlehem Temple, Randallstown, MD

The chasm between instruction and identity is bridged by the relationship of father and son. Telling someone what to do is different than telling them who they are. I'm grateful for the insights that Bishop Randy Borders shares in this "modern manual" for discovering the proper definition and balance between fathers and mentors. Our generation will be all the better as they engage this book!

L. Spenser Smith

Senior Pastor, Impact Nation Fellowship Church, Tuscaloosa, AL

Author, *Getting Ready for Love*

Bishop Randy Borders, whom I've known for three decades has written a masterpiece concerning "Fathering." His words are "apples of gold in pictures of Silver."

God creates originals, not photocopies. Templates, not duplicates. Yet, though the wheel is not new, it can be perfected. Such is life. Fathers are God's shortcut to success in life in ministry. Fatherlessness is a Brand marked "X." Mentors are a Brand making the "Next." Fathers represent visibly what God the Father is invisibly. Jehovah Jireh provides, so do Fathers. Nearly all the myriad of ascriptions applied to God, are also applicable to fathers. Jehovah Shammah: "God Who is Present" and so on.

Bishop Randy Borders has his finger on God's pulse. His stethoscope to God's heart. Fathers are associated with either "blessing or iniquity." Having no spiritual father often results in "no identity." This generation is the fatherless one. Therefore, it's imperative to turn the heart of fathers to children and the hearts of children to fathers. This will reverse the curse and stay the plague in the Church and upon the Street.

This book is for thinkers and feelers. It's difficult to heal what we can't feel. You can feel his words and they are anointed to heal. I highly recommend this concise, incise, and precise penning as an antidote to what plagues society and the Church. Mentoring, though named for mentor in mythology, is sound in theology and modeled in Christ-ology. "The difference between leaders and laity is the level of their thinking." Meta-Thinkers mold minds and create worlds. This Man of God, the anointed author, is such a man.

Bishop Brian Keith Williams

Brian Keith Williams Ministries, Orlando, FL

Once again, Bishop Randy Borders has provided a work that is so timely and on the pulse of what the world needs now! In my opinion, true fathering is a lost art in today's society. However, this book, *More than a Mentor,* helps to bring the essence of what true fathering is back to the forefront. Thank you, Bishop Borders, for sharing with the world the gift and treasure of your wisdom, insight, and grace that I have had the honor of experiencing first hand for the last 20 years! I am who I am because you were the Paul this Timothy needed! I am honored to be your son in the faith.

Mitchel D. Blue

Senior Pastor, UnCommon Church, Charlotte, NC

I want to dedicate this book to those on whose shoulders I now stand:

Pastor Larry Brooks (Young's Grove Missionary Baptist Church, Blacksburg, SC) took a chance on a teenage boy who felt the call of God on his life. He licensed and ordained me into ministry. Thank you for believing in me.

Bishop Brian Keith Williams, (All Nations Church, Columbus, OH) saw a gift in my life that was uncultivated and allowed me to travel the nation as a young budding pastor for four years. I learned how to develop an itinerate ministry; the importance of study; and the importance of Kingdom Connections.

Bishop Otis Lockett (Evangel COGIC, Greensboro, NC) served as my pastor from my second week in college in 1986 until the day of his passing October 12, 2012. The first time I heard him preach, something stood up in the eternity of my spirit and I knew it was my "father's voice." He taught us to seek lost souls and the importance of prayer, discipleship, and evangelism. Had Heaven not called him home, I'd still be sitting at the apostle's feet.

Bishop Cynthia R. James (The Potter's House, Dallas, TX), since the first time you invited me to cover your pulpit in Oakland, California, almost twenty years ago, our hearts have been knit together. I'm grateful for all the opportunities, insight, wisdom, encouragement, late-night talks, scolding, and rebukes. I'm a better husband and father because of the balance that you insisted I maintain. You taught me to engage the text. I haven't mastered it, but I do my best.

Bishop Kenneth Yelverton (Temple of Refuge International, Charlotte, NC). You've always been a big brother, helping me when I was wounded, giving clarity in my confusion, and lifting me when I was down. You make serving you easy. Though you didn't birth me, thank you for receiving me. I'll serve you as a son and pray I make you proud.

Harvest Church Ministries International, I thank you for the opportunity to serve and share the wisdom that I have gained through the years. You have constantly reminded me of my purpose.

Faith Harvest Church, you are my first church plant and my longest pastorate. Through the ups, the downs, the happiness, and the tears, you encouraged me to keep reaching for all that God has for me. For this I will forever be grateful.

Norma Borders, you are not only my wife of twenty-four years and the mother of my children, but you are my best friend. Thank you for loving me through the years and always pushing me to purpose. I am who I am today because of you. I love you now and always.

Efrim and Hope, thank you for releasing me to the world. You are the best kids a father could hope for.

CONTENTS

Foreword 3

A Note from the Author 6

Releasing Your Destiny 7

The Responsibilities of a Spiritual Father 9

The Responsibilities of the Sons and Daughters 55

Reuniting Father and Son 73

Notes 89

About the Author 91

About Sermon To Book 93

Foreword

I am the son of Dr. Frank Guns, Sr., both biologically and spiritually. Yet I am also the product of many great men and women whose words and example to this day continues to influence me. The man I am and the man I desire to be is the result of the imprint on my life. As I stroll through the pages of this groundbreaking book written by my brother Bishop Randy Borders I see my ministry journey delineated and describe both graphically and accurately. For like many who will read this book I understand the awkward balance of Spiritual Covering, both as the one covered and the one who covers. Bishop Borders does an amazing job of capturing this tension and speaking to both the father/mother and the children. His insightful interpretation of scripture opens the mind of the reader to see the familiar differently. His courageous approach to the difficult and sometimes misunderstood relationship between a spiritual parent and a son or daughter sheds new light for all to gain a clearer understanding. Understanding that many now are employing this relationship paradigm to define how pastors relate to each other and the pew, it's necessary to bring clarity. Clarity only occurs when honest engagement exists. This requires the minimization of egos and the embrace of humility which is a non-negotiable trait. The value of a godly connection then must never be devalued and those who appropriately manage the relationship will enjoy immeasurable benefits both personally and professionally. That's why we need books like this that deconstructs while reconstructing at the same time. Note as well that this reconstruction does more than utilize the same material but ultimately gives a new expression which allows each generation of Spiritual leadership to continue to flourish. In essence, the relationship such as David to Mephibosheth, Bishop Borders reconstructs it, so the reader sees differently and now has greater clarity as to what adoption looks like.

More than a Mentor will stretch you beyond the bounds of traditional thinking and cause you to wrestle with how you as either a Spiritual Parent or Spiritual child maintain healthy relationships. With so much perceived abuse within the Body of Christ, it's necessary that healthy dialogue occurs. This involves dealing with tough and sometimes uncomfortable topics such as what Bishop Borders willingly addresses. Topics such as what is Spiritual covering and what are the differences between spiritual leadership and fleshly loyalty paramount in today's church culture. As the church navigates its way through the uncharted waters of the 21st century with its myriad of social, religious, and political issues, it is of the utmost importance that we seek to deal frankly with mentorship and parenthood within today's church.

I appreciate Bishop Border's life commitment to this topic and I am certain that all who reads this will be inspired and informed. For as we press to become a more effective church, the work of Bishop Borders will be profoundly important.

As you read this wonderful book, enter into conversation with others and create forums of discussion. You, your peers, and your partners will be better. Enjoy the journey of becoming more than a mentor.

Dr. John E Guns
Senior Pastor, Saint Paul Church of Jacksonville, Inc
Jacksonville, Florida
Author, Journey to Wholeness

A Note from the Author

Welcome!

As you read *More than a Mentor*, you will notice that a workbook section, including reflective questions and an application-oriented action step, follows each chapter. These questions and action steps are included to help you better understand and appreciate the role of spiritual fathers in the church and in your spiritual life.

In addition to the space provided to record your responses to each question, you'll find a notes page at the end of each workbook section for jotting down additional responses and thoughts.

May this book help you to grow in your relationship with your spiritual parents, your sons and daughters, and above all, your heavenly Father.

– *Bishop Randy Borders*

INTRODUCTION

Releasing Your Destiny

At the time of writing this book, I have served as an itinerant speaker for over thirty years, a senior pastor for twenty-eight years, and a consecrated bishop for twenty-two years. The message I share in this book is one dear to my heart. Why? Because, first, I believe many of us never recognize the blessing of a genuine connection to an authentic spiritual leader. And, second, many of us never maximize the benefit of a legitimate, God-ordained spiritual covering. As a result, we are heir to blessings and benefits we never receive.

> *And no one takes the honor to himself, but receives it when he is called by God, even as Aaron was.* — ***Hebrews 5:4 (NASB)***

Real spiritual fathers are not intimidated or frightened by the gifts they encounter. In fact, they search for and seek out gifts destined for greatness, but in need of great instruction. They have the uncanny ability to discern your weaknesses, foresee your pitfalls, and point you in a direction that is healthy, holy, and wholesome. Authentic Kingdom fathers are confident in their own anointing. They see their mission as truly cultivating, protecting, and caring for those to whom they are called.

Yet, for many, it's hard to see their pastor beyond just being their preacher. I often say, if you see him or her as only your preacher, then the only thing you will reap is a sermon, but if you see them as your prophet, you will always reap a word from the Lord. If you see them as your father, you will understand the love. You will comprehend their need to prepare you, and you will appreciate their correction and direction as a necessary part of reaching your God-given purpose. They are destiny-releasers.

There is a difference between the person who merely teaches you and the one who is ordained to push you into purpose. There is a difference between the person who merely trains you and the one who releases you into your ministry. My prayer is that after reading this book, you won't see your leader as a mere man or woman, but that you would place a demand on the treasure God has placed within them for you. For they are, truly, more than a mentor.

> *But we have this treasure in earthen vessels, so that the surpassing greatness of the power will be of God and not from ourselves... —* ***2 Corinthians 4:7 (NASB)***

CHAPTER ONE

The Responsibilities of a Spiritual Father

By faith Noah, when warned about things not yet seen, in holy fear built an ark to save his family. By his faith he condemned the world and became heir of the righteousness that is in keeping with faith. — ***Hebrews 11:7 (NIV)***

To understand the message of this book, you have to understand a hermeneutic law that says, "Every scripture has both a literal meaning and a spiritual meaning."[1] Naturally, Jesus healed blinded eyes. Spiritually, some of us couldn't see where we were until we gave our lives to Christ. The natural and spiritual are parallel truths. The Apostle Paul, a Father to many, spoke of first the natural, then the spiritual. In the original creation, it was first the spiritual (the Word), then the natural (Creation).

Hebrews 11:7 is layered with such truths. So, let's look at what this text teaches us.

When the anger of God had grown hot against humanity, God chose a man to preach His message of salvation to the world. The man he chose was a father, given the instruction to build a structure that would house every kind of living creation. He was instructed about a rain and a judgment coming, and told to build an ark of safety.

Noah's ministry assignment was to create a solution for a problem that had yet to arise. This unique assignment made him ridiculed by his peers and misunderstood by his community. God often raises up men and calls them to raise up others to be an answer before the problem ever arises. This takes a special grace.

Noah's sons, who themselves never heard from God, had to trust their father's relationship with God and build according to the pattern God gave their father. We never see God telling the sons or their wives about the blueprint. God never gives the sons dimensions, and neither did he tell them what rain looked or smelled like. God used a wise father who found grace in His sight to lead his sons to build a multi-dimensional, multicultural structure, strong enough to withstand the heaviest storm the earth had experienced.

God could have just chosen a preacher or a prophet, but the writer of the book of Hebrews accentuates he is a father, moving with a holy fear, building to "save his family." Noah wasn't really trying to save the world as much he was trying to save his family. I'm sure over the 120 years of Noah's preaching career, his sons got tired of building, got frustrated with delay, and got discouraged because of the community's disregard for their futuristic message. But, they stayed loyal to their dad and helped him build a legacy of faith that literally ushered a current generation to a place where they would reproduce again. They were afforded the opportunity to see their father patient in his process, so they were resilient enough to bounce back after life's most vicious storm had destroyed all they had previously known. This earned them a place eternally etched in history.

I've been the father of two amazing children, Efrim and Hope, for a number of years. I provide emotional, financial, and spiritual support to my children. I have seen my children at their best and at their worst. I have coached them through difficult days and congratulated them on monumental occasions.

Like most parents, I take my responsibilities seriously. It is *my job* to point my children in the direction of destiny. Sometimes, I correct them. Other times, I encourage them. But at all times, I love them.

Being a father is more than a responsibility, it is a calling. The reason I take my job so seriously is because I know the absence of a father in the life of a child can do more damage than good. A poor relationship with one's father can be devastating to that child's future. My role is crucial to my children's well-being and the development of *their* callings.

It is not a job I take lightly. It's actually quite sobering.

Now that I am a pastor, I see a need for the same kind of nurturing to be done for the people I lead. Whether they are members of my church or pastors affiliated with and connected to our network, I see an important need to "father" my spiritual children the way I father my natural children.

Train up a child in the way he should go, and when he is old he will not depart from it. — ***Proverbs 22:6 (NKJV)***

It is my duty to help others learn how to pray, how to rely on God, and how to both discover and uncover their spiritual gifts. It is my duty to encourage them toward holiness and dissuade them from destructive spiritual behavior.

And just like fathering my biological children, being a father to my spiritual sons and daughters is one of the most important things in my life. Every true father wants to see their children advance and go further in life than they did.

All throughout Scripture, several passages point to the importance of spiritual parenting which goes beyond simple mentorship.

Elisha was fathered spiritually by Elijah (2 Kings 2:9–12). Joshua was trained by and received spiritual impartation from Moses (Numbers 27:18–20; Joshua 1:1). Naomi reared Ruth, even though Ruth was sent to help Naomi (Ruth 1:1–22). Mary was, for a season, developed by Elizabeth (Luke 1:54–57), and Jesus most certainly fathered his twelve disciples (John 5:19). As Jesus mimicked his father, he expected them to mimic him.

The importance of spiritual parenting in the community of faith is so clear in scripture, yet in modern-day America, we tend to live a very singular life. We tend to think our direct connection to God is the only thing we need to be developed spiritually. And we are less likely to have a spiritual leader to whom we connect for covenantal accountability, wise counsel, and ministerial affirmation.

But I am here to tell you we are missing out. Every single person who follows Christ needs a spiritual parent who mentors, loves, and nurtures as much like every single baby born today needs a natural father who will be there day in and day out.

So, what does the role of a spiritual father look like? What are the responsibilities and what are the boundaries?

The goal of this book is to briefly define, explain, and contextualize the roles and the responsibilities of a spiritual father and shed light on how spiritual "children" can support these leaders in a mutually beneficial relationship that gives glory to God. We hear a lot about what sons ought to do for the father, but not enough about what the fathers ought to do for the sons.

What Is a Spiritual Father?

Just as babies are born into an environment, believers are birthed into purpose. Every son owes his existence to a father. Somebody taught him or her the scriptures. Somebody mentored them into purpose. Somebody gave them an opportunity to use their gift. Somebody gave them a chance or a platform.

Natural children carry their father's DNA (deoxyribonucleic acid). DNA is the carrier of genetic information, causing attributes of the father to show up in the children. Spiritual fathers pass on spiritual DNA. You often see the ways, mannerisms, habits, and sometimes even the style in the sons and daughters. I have said many times mentors leave you with blueprints, while fathers leave you with imprints (DNA). Mentors give information while fathers give impartation. Fathers impart life and legacy.

I do want to be clear concerning this DNA issue. Just because you receive an impartation from a ministry or get saved under that ministry, it doesn't make them a father in the truest sense. As in the natural, there is a difference between a sperm-donor and a father, and so it is in the spiritual. A father takes the time to make clear to you your path and speaks to your future, not just to your history. He helps you understand your spiritual lineage, spiritual pedigree, and spiritual authority.

A spiritual father is someone who provides spiritual oversight, insight, care, counsel, correction, and direction to individuals to whom God has assigned them.

A spiritual father is a guide.

A spiritual father is a coach.

A spiritual father is a counselor.

A spiritual father is a caregiver.

A spiritual father is a listener.

A spiritual father is a disciplinarian.

A spiritual father is a teacher.

A spiritual father is an example.

Spiritual fathers are most often senior pastors, but they are not exclusively pastors.

Spiritual fathers may be mentors, professors, teachers, ministers, or counselors, helping Christ-followers to become all that God has called them to become. Though they may serve in these capacities, a spiritual father is so much more than a mentor.

For the purposes of this book, I will use the term "father" interchangeably with "spiritual father" when talking about someone who births you into purpose, who provides experience and wisdom, who fosters encouragement, and who is a living, Christlike example to others. But in no way are women isolated from this spiritual responsibility!

While there is sufficient evidence in Scripture that speaks to "sonship" specifically, and the role a father has with respect to his sons and daughters, we also see women like Junia, listed as a female apostle in Romans16:7. Her ministry stood out so to the apostle Paul he called her a "co-laborer" and a "noted apostle." I do not intend to exclude women from the call. I believe this can be for everyone, and the call to mentor, rear, and raise up God's children in the admonition of the Lord is not just for men.

Everyone needs to be mentored. Everyone needs to be fathered or mothered. Everyone needs to have a connection with someone who knows him or her both on and off the stage. My pastor, the late Bishop Otis Lockett, Sr., used to ask us pastors, "Who can rebuke you? Who can talk to you about the pitfalls that you are heading toward? Who can talk to you about your marriage?" Every believer needs a shepherd, and every shepherd needs a shepherd (Numbers 27:16–17). To be in authority, you need to be under authority (Matthew 8:7–10).

How Does It Work?

One of the greatest biblical examples of a spiritual father is of Eli to Samuel. In 1 Samuel, a woman by the name of Hannah was barren. In response, she prayed:

> *In her deep anguish Hannah prayed to the LORD, weeping bitterly. And she made a vow, saying, "LORD Almighty, if you will only look on your servant's misery and remember me, and not forget your servant but give her a son, then I will give him to the LORD for all the days of his life, and no razor will ever be used on his head."* — **1 Samuel 1:10–11 (NIV)**

Hannah promised to give her child to God so he might be reared in the knowledge of God. And very soon after, she conceived. Later in the text, baby Samuel was born, but instead of bringing him to his earthly father, Hannah brought him to his spiritual father, a prophet by the name of Eli.

Eli was a high priest in the temple, and he accepted the responsibility to raise Samuel in the tutelage of the Lord—he accepted the role of spiritual father.

As such, Eli trained Samuel on temple worship. He taught Samuel to discern the voice of the Lord. The voice of the Lord to Samuel sounded like his spiritual father, Eli. Many times, God sounds like our leaders because our leaders echo the mind of God. Eli remained in Samuel's life throughout his ministry tenure to give advice and sound counsel on all things appertaining to a priestly, God-first lifestyle. Though Eli himself made some grave errors concerning sin that he did not correct, he taught Samuel well. Samuel went on to live an incredible life for God—something that might not have happened without Eli's input and direction.

Just as I had nothing to do with choosing my biological parents, so with my spiritual parents. It was God's choice. So it is with spiritual fathers. We don't shop for fathers, choosing who has the best preaching style or the largest church or the most popularity. God makes the choice for you and alerts you to the one that He has called you to. You may see something in them you admire, but God, by His Spirit, will connect you with the leader who will bring you into purpose. It's a God-thing.

> *God setteth the solitary in families.* — ***Psalm 68:6 (KJV)***

> *But now God has set the members, each one of them, in the body just as He pleased.* — ***I Corinthians 12:18 (NKJV)***

The scripture seems to differentiate between an offspring and a son. In Isaiah 9:6, the scripture says, "For unto us a child is born, unto us a son is given."

This suggest that a child or offspring is *born,* but a son is *processed*. Jesus is born as a child or offspring in the manger, but he is only "given" as a *son* after he has gone through years of obedience to the father. He enters into ministry at thirty-three years of age as a *son*.

Now, a spiritual father is not the only individual who can minister to you, but much like the example of Eli and Samuel, he or she is the appointed person from God responsible for helping you to reach your ultimate, God-given purpose.

Without spiritual fathers, sons and daughters of the gospel would wander without direction.

Without spiritual fathers, children would be filled with zeal and excitement, but they would lack clarity and wisdom.

A true spiritual parent is selfless. A true spiritual parent does not withhold helpful criticisms from his or her child. They are straightforward in a loving way. They correct. They uplift. And their greatest joy is to see their child win. Their greatest blessing is to experience their child living his or her best life.

Fathers understand their call is not to be their sons' best friends, but rather to equip them for adulthood. It is a joy to watch your natural son or daughter develop, grow, and experience life, but there's always a danger when you allow your children to think they are on the same level that you are on. Becoming too "common" can lead to the disrespect of your life's assignment, which is to bring them to maturity.

I believe spiritual fathers are charged with a God-given responsibility to give us the tools we need to succeed, and they will not stop until we have achieved all God has placed in our hearts.

The Covering Is Anointed

> *Moreover, the LORD spoke to Moses, saying, "Take also for yourself the finest of spices: of flowing myrrh five hundred shekels, and of fragrant cinnamon half as much, two*

hundred and fifty, and of fragrant cane two hundred and fifty, and of cassia five hundred, according to the shekel of the sanctuary, and of olive oil a hin. You shall make of these a holy anointing oil, a perfume mixture, the work of a perfumer; it shall be a holy anointing oil. With it you shall anoint the tent of meeting and the ark of the testimony, and the table and all its utensils, and the lampstand and its utensils, and the altar of incense, and the altar of burnt offering and all its utensils, and the laver and its stand. You shall also consecrate them, that they may be most holy; whatever touches them shall be holy. You shall anoint Aaron and his sons, and consecrate them, that they may minister as priests to Me. You shall speak to the sons of Israel, saying, 'This shall be a holy anointing oil to Me throughout your generations. It shall not be poured on anyone's body, nor shall you make any like it in the same proportions; it is holy, and it shall be holy to you. Whoever shall mix any like it or whoever puts any of it on a layman shall be cut off from his people.'" — ***Exodus 30:22–33 (NASB)***

The level of detail in this passage shows how important it was that God-appointed things and God-appointed leaders be anointed. The list of ingredients is unique and metaphorical.

Myrrh is bitter. It represents the tough experiences God allows to come into one's life. Cinnamon is full of flavor, very distinct. This represents the good days and happy moments. Sugar is sweet. It is representational of life's epic moments and monumental occasions. Cassia is a dried flower, which has meaning when you think about how God lets some things bloom one day and dry up the next.[2] He does all of this as part of stirring up the anointing for your life.

The final ingredient was a hin of anointed oil, which means about 3-2/3 liters.[3] The oil represented the Holy

Spirit. This is saying no matter what you have experienced, there will be more of the presence and Spirit of God in your life than good or bad days you have experienced.

According to the passage, the mixture was to be applied to the priests' garments. He was specific to point out the anointing compound was not to go on the flesh. It wasn't his flesh or humanity being anointed, it was his garment or his covering. No matter how close the Lord allows you to get to a man or woman of God, never forget their flesh is *not* anointed. Don't seek to know your leader after the flesh (2 Corinthians 5:16).

We do our spiritual fathers a disservice by not recognizing they are human as we are. Hebrews 5:1 says, "For every high priest taken from among men is appointed for men in things pertaining to God, that he may offer both gifts and sacrifices for sins" (NKJV).

Though the spiritual fathers themselves are fallible beings, the "covering" they wear is anointed by God.

Dr. Cynthia James says, "If we are honest people, we recognize that we could never deserve what the Lord has done for us. We didn't earn it or merit it. If no one else knows, we know. We know who we really are."[4]

This reflects the story in Luke 8:43–48 of the woman who had bled for twelve years. She only had to touch the garment ("covering") of Jesus and she was healed. She didn't need a counseling session or to know the names of all the disciples. She said within herself, "If I can just touch the hem of his covering, I will be made whole." She touched Jesus' covering and was immediately made well.

As for the process of anointing people, Psalm 133 says the oil flows from the head down to the fringes of the garment. Furthermore, it was reserved for priests and their descendants.

Today, we revere pastors as having an anointing. They are the special individuals called by God and given a vision of the church and of what God wants us to do here on earth. Because the senior pastor is the authority figure in the local church, he or she represents the head. The oil of anointing flows from the senior pastor down to the congregation.

> *Let your garments always be white, And let your head lack no oil.* — ***Ecclesiastes 9:8 (NKJV)***

As with your natural body, it takes the spiritual body (arms and hands) to pour oil on the head. It takes a praying church body to intercede for God's presence to be on their leader.

> *So the Lord said to Moses: "Gather to Me seventy men of the elders of Israel, whom you know to be the elders of the people and officers over them; bring them to the tabernacle of meeting, that they may stand there with you. Then I will come down and talk with you there. I will take of the Spirit that is upon you and will put the same upon them; and they shall bear the burden of the people with you, that you may not bear it yourself alone."* — ***Numbers 11:16–17 (NKJV)***

God raised up Moses as a spiritual father to Israel. He took the Spirit, the grace, and the anointing he had mantled Moses with and transferred them to the people at the laying on of Moses' hands.

In Numbers 11:26–27, Eldad and Medad were *not* elders, but they prophesied. When the elders had hands laid on them, they prophesied. God took of the Spirit that was upon Moses and put on the elders. He took the same anointing and transferred that to them. They "prophesied" because Deuteronomy 34:10 says, "There had no *prophet* risen like Moses." They had their leader's heart and spirit. It's not going to happen just because you fast and pray. It's going to happen when you submit to and come under the hands of your leader.

Joshua saw Medad and Eldad prophesying and said, let's stop them from prophesying! He didn't understand that even though they didn't have hands laid on them by Moses, they had relationship with the elders who had received their leader's spirit.

Elders have to understand that their job is *not* to represent themselves. They are to take of the anointing they have received and transfer that to the body. The pastor is like *the head* and the elders and leadership are like *the neck.* The head can be sending the right signal, but if there is a neck injury, the body is paralyzed.

Most of the time when we have church-problems, it's not as much as a pastor's problem as much as it is a leadership problem. People follow a pastor because they like where he's going, but if you want to know where the church is going, look at those who walk closest to him.

A pastor is going to go up whether the church goes up or not, but many churches don't grow with their pastor because the leadership is not hooked up and connected with the pastor. There are so many agendas and so many ulterior motives that you can't see a move of God. Your father's mantle is important to your destiny.

Much like the priest's anointing flowed to his descendants (Leviticus 8:30), a spiritual father's anointing flows to those under him.

In Genesis 49, Jacob did not die until he called his sons together and told them what would happen in the end times. He told them about their inheritance. He gave them instructions. His sons would have missed out on all of this had they cut him out of their lives.

Your relationship with your spiritual father is so important. The oil flows down. Once you break your connection and reject your anointed leader and father in ministry, you are rejecting blessing and anointing on your own life.

My spiritual father, Otis Lockett, Sr., always told us that when God wants to birth a destiny, He first births a relationship. Don't allow new relationships that come in your life to cause you to forget your ordained connection. The devil respects the spiritual covering of your leader. That mantle should be on your life as well.[5]

The Law of Supply and Demand

Now a certain woman had a flow of blood for twelve years, and had suffered many things from many physicians. She had spent all that she had and was no better, but rather grew worse. When she heard about Jesus, she came behind Him in the crowd and touched His garment. For she said, "If only I may touch His clothes, I shall be made well." Immediately the fountain of her blood was

> *dried up, and she felt in her body that she was healed of the affliction. And Jesus, immediately knowing in Himself that power had gone out of Him, turned around in the crowd and said, "Who touched My clothes?" But His disciples said to Him, "You see the multitude thronging You, and You say, 'Who touched Me?'" And He looked around to see her who had done this thing. But the woman, fearing and trembling, knowing what had happened to her, came and fell down before Him and told Him the whole truth. —* ***Mark 5:25–33 (NKJV)***

Let's examine Mark's account of the woman with the issue of blood. In my book, *The Adjutant's Guide to Etiquette,* I discuss something called the Law of Supply and Demand. Where there is a demand, there will always be a supply. The same law works with spiritual things. When you, by faith, put a spiritual demand on the spiritual leader God has placed over you, they will always have something for you. You will be receiving while your leader isn't even aware. Like the woman with the issue of blood, Jesus wasn't trying to give her anything in particular. She just "took it" from his presence. When you are around a chosen vessel, there is more "caught" than "taught." There are things I now do just like my pastor. He never taught me. I got the impartation from his covering.

> *And the whole multitude sought to touch Him, for power went out from Him and healed them all. —* ***Luke 6:19 (NKJV)***

There it is again—*the law of supply and demand.*

> *But Jesus said to them, "A prophet is not without honor except in his own country, among his own relatives, and in his own house." Now He could do no mighty work there, except that He laid His hands on a few sick people and healed them. And He marveled because of their unbelief. Then He went about the villages in a circuit, teaching.*
> — ***Mark 6:4–6 (NKJV)***

Notice this is the same Jesus, but because these hometown people were familiar with him, they missed what the others received by just getting close to his covering. Their perception of him hindered what he was able to do. He had revolutionary power available, but because they couldn't perceive who he was, it was not available to them. You have to perceive the greatness in your leader and the greatness in your connection to them. If you perceive him as just a righteous man you get a righteous man's reward, but if you perceive him as a prophet, you can get a prophet's reward (Matthew 10:41). The woman with the issue of blood perceived his covering was anointed, and when she touched it, she was immediately healed.

In the life of Joseph, he receives three primary garments or coverings. The first was the "coat of favor" given by his father. The second coat he received was in Potiphar's house. This coat indicated he was over all the house. Then he received a coat in prison. I know this is true because when Pharaoh called him out of prison, he changed his garment. Pharaoh brought him out of prison and gave him a ring, chain, and a royal garment. At every juncture in his life, it seems the enemy was fighting to get his covering. The significance of Pharaoh's garment is that he told Joseph when he put this covering on, that "only in the throne would Joseph be second to him." It wasn't merely Joseph's coat. It was Pharaoh's garment of authority.

When you step out with your leader, you are honored because they are honored. Never be confused to think that you are more than you are. People respect you because of your connection with your leader. Wear the coat and covering of your leader with grace and humility. Blessings flow through them to you, simply because you are submitted to your leadership and desire to serve.

In 2 Kings 4, there is a Shunammite woman who perceives that Elijah is a holy man of God. She and her husband built a room onto their home as a gift to him. The prophet prophesies that she will have a son in a year from the date. She has a son, and he gets older. One day he is in the field plowing and has a heat stroke. He eventually dies. In verse 19, she lays him on the bed of the prophet. The bed has his covers, or his covering. She put the thing that had been birthed as a result of prophecy back under the prophet's "covering." She went and got the prophet (the original word), and the boy revived.

Elisha just poured water on the hands of the man of God. He served his pastor Elijah. He stayed with him and would not leave. When Elijah was taken up on a chariot, his mantle-garment came down. This cloth was his covering. This carried the same miracle-working power that his spiritual father walked in. Elisha takes the mantle-covering of his father in the gospel and does twice as many miracles in his lifetime than his father, Elijah.

Paul sent out handkerchiefs and aprons from his body. These garments carried the authority of his apostolic covering. The sick were healed and demons were cast out. This was not just “fabric” or “cloth.” This was a sign that his apostolic covering had reached the region. The devil had to recognize his apostolic covering wherever it showed up.

Jesus could not come into ministry until the Holy Spirit descended on him. That was a type of garment of the Father. Even upon Jesus’ death, sinners at the foot of the cross argued over his natural covering. I don’t think it was just because it was seamless, for they had seen the garments of kings. I believe that there was something so special about his covering that they would not even tear it. They cast lots for it. They might not have known what was so different about his covering, but they all wanted to take it home with them. It’s all about covering.

In the state of North Carolina, you may not be an electrician, but if you want to do electrical work, you can find someone who has a license and work under their license number. Many times, we don’t have a third of the qualifications needed to serve the leaders that God places us under. God allows us to get up under their “number,” as it were, and go to work. We serve under a garment of authority that belongs to another man. Let us realize that we are successful and effective because we have found the order of God, submitting ourselves to one greater in the kingdom.

Spiritual Fathers Help Us Find Our Identity

In the Old Testament, one of the jobs of any father was to take his child into the temple on the boy's eighth day to be circumcised. During the moment of circumcision, the child received his name after the father cut back his flesh. The removal of the flesh represented the cutting away of everything that was unnecessary for the male reproduction when that time came. After the cutting back of the flesh, the boy was to receive his God-ordained identity.[6]

It's important to note God entrusted the man's natural father to cut away the flesh of his son as a sign of his covenant with God. It was the *father* who had to make sure this was done. It was the *father* who God relied on.

In the same way, God entrusts spiritual fathers to cut back what is unnecessary and help guide us toward our identity in Christ. Fathers can't be so enamored with the giftedness of their sons and daughters that they don't deal with the issues that they see such as pride, greed, selfishness, cynicism, dishonesty, laziness, pretention, et cetera.

Spiritual fathers are sensitive and stern. They are sensitive enough to recognize the carnal parts of you needing to be cut away and stern enough to perform spiritual surgery if necessary. Spiritual fathers are used by God to remove the layers distracting you from your God-ordained purpose.

Your identity is important to God. Who you are is important to God. Jesus's identity was so important the Father made an appearance while Jesus was being baptized to announce, "This is My beloved Son, in whom I am well pleased" (Matthew 3:17 NASB).

In the same way circumcision in the Old Testament could be viewed as an "identity marker" for males in covenant with God, baptism may be viewed as another identity marker to those who confess Jesus Christ as Lord. It is an outward sign of an inward commitment. Every spiritual father is going to encourage you to take this step of obedience to live a life separated unto God. You are God's property and your life's call is to do His Will.

In Joshua 5, the children of Israel are on the brink of crossing the Jordan, but before they cross, Joshua gets a command from God. Something has to happen before Israel can go into their promised land. Joshua has to make the mark of circumcision.

> *At that time the LORD said to Joshua, "Make for yourself flint knives and circumcise again the sons of Israel the second time." So, Joshua made himself flint knives and circumcised the sons of Israel at Gibeath-haaraloth. This is the reason why Joshua circumcised them: all the people who came out of Egypt who were males, all the men of war, died in the wilderness along the way after they came out of Egypt. For all the people who came out were circumcised, but all the people who were born in the wilderness along the way as they came out of Egypt had not been circumcised. For the sons of Israel walked forty years in the wilderness, until all the nation, that is, the men of war who came out of Egypt, perished because they did not listen to the voice of the LORD, to whom the LORD had sworn that He would not let them see the land which the LORD had sworn to their fathers to give us, a land flowing with milk and honey. Their children whom He raised up in their place, Joshua circumcised; for they were*

uncircumcised, because they had not circumcised them along the way. — ***Joshua 5:2–7(NASB)***

This happens at a point when Moses, who had been a father to the nation of Israel, had died. Before God allows Israel to possess their new territory, He uses a man of God to circumcise them a second time. It is important to note these are not small children being circumcised, but these are grown men. The "extra flesh" that they carried had become a part of who they were all their lives. They are now faced with the decision of letting go of what had become a part of them. As they got close to occupying their destined place, these men who were twenty years old and upward had to trust God's man to handle a very private part of them. The cutting is in a "private place." They opened up an intimate area and let God's man deal with that part of them.

There must be mutual trust. The father has to show his sensitivity and care as a father, and the son has to show his vulnerability to submit as a son. They both had to trust each other. They had to literally trust t Joshua would not castrate them or render them unable to reproduce again. Spiritual fathers have to be careful they do not cut too deep or rebuke too sharply. It is their job to make sure the sons are able to reproduce spiritually, when they come to that season of their lives.

The men who followed Joshua had to trust that Joshua's mark to their flesh was representative of covenant and not an attempt at castration. The men who let Joshua circumcise them were in essence saying their hearts were with Joshua and that they now trusted him as they did his spiritual father, Moses.

When fathers have to deal with sons on serious matters that could make shipwrecks of their lives, they mustn't do it simply because they *can*, but rather because they *care*. Sons have to be willing to take the cut to make the cut. I've had several such incidents on my journey.

When I was a young minister, I received an invitation to preach at a neighboring church. The protocol was that when we received an invitation to preach, we got the approval to go out from our pastor. We were free to go minister, but if we were having service at our home church, pastor required for us to take care of home and be in service.

It just so happened that my engagement fell on a church night. I accepted the invitation without approval of my pastor and secretly informed about twenty people in our young adult group that we would be meeting at the church and traveling to my preaching engagement. The evening came for the engagement. We all arrived at church, loaded up in cars, and proceeded to form a caravan to travel to my engagement.

Just before we were ready to pull out, one of the elders of the church came and knocked on my window and told me that I was needed inside. I tried to explain how going inside would make me late for my engagement, knowing all the while that my caravan was out of order. We knew the guidelines for ministry, but I refused to go through the proper channels because I was so ambitious and wanted to preach so badly. I saw a "no" as an insult to who I was.

Upon entering the church, Bishop Otis Lockett, Sr., invited me to the front row to have a seat. Actually, it was me and all those who had attempted to go with me. He gently reminded me of the standard. He proceeded to preach exactly what he had intended to preach without mentioning me in his message, but I had to sit there and make myself smile. It was such a blow to my pride.

It was hard to hold my head up, but I knew all the while the way that I had attempted to go out to minister was wrong. I could have chosen to be offended at the "cut," but instead, I chose to humble myself, endure the embarrassment, and amend my ways. Truthfully, I think my father in ministry saw pride and rebellion that I didn't know I had. Today, I am so glad that he was not afraid to deal with the prideful, arrogant Randy Borders. That guy was *gifted*, but *not ready*. The "cut" then was necessary for me to experience the success I am having today. Yes, I admit I've messed up a lot along my journey and had to have my actions and motives checked. I can walk in humility and servitude today because someone was bold enough to tell me that it's not about me, but it's about the people I'm called to love and the assignment that God has given me.

Paul also had a spiritual son named Timothy (this is revealed throughout 1 and 2 Timothy), but Timothy could not come into his own personal ministry until he submitted to Paul as his spiritual father and covering. From what we know, Timothy had been taught the Scriptures by his mother and grandmother, but he could not be fully released into what God had for his ministry until he came under the hand of his spiritual father, Paul. Timothy receives an impartation at the hands of Paul. Paul becomes the channel through which the current flows. Timothy submits to Paul as a spiritual son (1 Timothy 1:18).

Through mentorship, Timothy became the pastor at the church at Ephesus, which grew to 100,000 under his leadership. It's an incredible look at how Paul helped Timothy find his identity and live up to his fullest potential in Christ. He actually had more people under his leadership than his father in ministry, but he was only able to get to that point because of the impartation he received from the Apostle Paul. Timothy never forgot the one who God used to identify his gifting's and set him apart.

How much could be ours, how would our identity be different if we connected to and followed the spiritual father, anointed by God, over our lives?

The Father's Honor

Ephesians 6:1–2, tells us that our natural, earthly parents deserve honor. It stands to reason, then, our spiritual parents deserve the same.

Honor is a biblical term with several meanings, but for the purposes of this book, I want to define honor as "expressing appreciation for." One way that we express appreciation for someone who does something for us or who pours something into us is by sowing financial seed or giving money to them. Honor is connected to money at least thirty times in the scripture.

Honour the LORD with thy substance, and with the firstfruits of all thine increase... — ***Proverbs 3:9 (KJV)***

But if you declare the dream and its interpretation, you will receive from me gifts and a reward and great honor; therefore declare to me the dream and its interpretation. ***— Daniel 2:6 (NASB)***

Let the elders who rule well be counted worthy of double honor, especially those who labor in the word and doctrine. — ***1 Timothy 5:17 (NKJV)***

In Romans 13:7 there is a list of those we are told to give their dues. There is listed tribute, custom, fear and honor. We are told by God to give Honor to whom honor is due. The word "honor" means valuables, i.e., money paid, and by analogy, esteem (especially of the highest degrees) or dignity. The word is also translated "precious."[7]

Perhaps you are accustomed to receiving a card on your birthday with money in it? If so, then you know the money inside of the card is not payment or compensation. The money represents honor. It is emblematic of one's appreciation for the care, concern, and counsel that the card's recipient has freely given.

Money is a symbol that quickly communicates appreciation and honor. Whenever someone works on a job and they get paid at the end of the week, the paycheck is for forty hours of their life given in work, sweat, and creativity. Money then represents life. When you sow money, you are actually giving a portion of your life back to the person whom you are honoring.

Some cards do not have money included in them, but the words expressed on the card, and the consideration given to that person is enough to say, "I see you. I value you, and I appreciate you and all you have done." Focus on making your leader feel honored and appreciate him or her for the work.

> *Then some Pharisees and teachers of the law came to Jesus from Jerusalem and asked, "Why do your disciples break the tradition of the elders? They don't wash their hands before they eat!"*
>
> *Jesus replied, "And why do you break the command of God for the sake of your tradition? For God said, 'Honor your father and mother' and 'Anyone who curses their father or mother is to be put to death.' But you say that if anyone declares that what might have been used to help their father or mother is 'devoted to God,' they are not to 'honor their father or mother' with it. Thus you nullify the word of God for the sake of your tradition.* — ***Matthew 15:1–6 (NIV)***

In Matthew 15, the word used for honor is *tima*. *Tima* comes from *timaó*, which means to assign value and to give honor.[8] This double meaning of both affixing value to something or someone *and* revering or honoring that thing or person comes full circle in this text.

In the text, the Pharisees were withholding value from their parents, claiming those items and honor were "devoted to God." They were saying that the money and the honor they would give was already spoken for or already devoted to a cause. It would be as if someone asked you to give to a charity and you say, "I already gave at the office." So, they were dodging a commandment for the sake of their man-made traditions.

> *Yet it was good of you to share in my troubles. Moreover, as you Philippians know, in the early days of your acquaintance with the gospel, when I set out from Macedonia, not one church shared with me in the matter of giving and receiving, except you only; for even when I was in Thessalonica, you sent me aid more than once when I was in need. Not that I desire your gifts; what I desire is that more be credited to your account. I have received full payment and have more than enough. I am amply supplied, now that I have received from Epaphroditus the gifts you sent. They are a fragrant offering, an acceptable sacrifice, pleasing to God. And my God will meet all your needs according to the riches of his glory in Christ Jesus.* — ***Philippians 4:14–19 (NIV)***

We love to quote Philippians 4:19 which says, "God will supply all your needs," but we fail to realize the promise was given to the Philippian church because they supported Paul. Paul said there was no other church shared with him concerning giving and receiving but Philippi. When you take care of God's servant, God promises to take care of you.

There are those who fight the entire concept of honoring spiritual fathers and they primarily use Matthew 23 to defend their position.

> *And call no man your father upon the earth: for one is your Father, which is in heaven.* — ***Matthew 23:9 (KJV)***

"Call no man your father upon the earth" isn't teaching it's wrong to acknowledge fathers, because the fifth commandment teaches us to honor our father. Scripture doesn't contradict itself. Nor is any scripture of private interpretation. In fact, scripture interprets itself, as it is rightly divided and compared with other scripture (2 Timothy 2:15). The context of the text reveals its contents.

The Pharisees believed and taught that the "teacher or master" was a father—the "maker of the man." One of the compound names of God is Jehovah-Hosenu: the Lord thy Maker. Only God is the Maker. Only God is the source of mankind's origin, not man. So, this verse means to "ascribe to no man the honor that is solely God's, as Creator and Maker.

Therefore, both Natural and Spiritual fathers deserve honor, but, only the Heavenly Father deserves the glory as the source of origin, existence, sustenance, and maintenance.

Satan loves to use irreverence and disrespect to gain a seat in our God-given connections and relationships. Remember, God gains His seat in reverence.

> *And Thou art holy, sitting in the Praise of Israel.* — ***Psalms 22:3 (YLT)***

On the other hand, Satan takes his seat in irreverence.

> *I know where you live, where the throne of Satan sits...* — ***Revelation 2:13 (BSB)***

One way Satan gains access into our God-given connections is through the spirit of irreverence. In so many cases, the irreverence toward the man or woman of God is indicative of their relationship with God.

The eighteenth-century poet Alexander Pope first penned the line, "Damn with faint praise, assent with civil leer."[9] If someone damns something with *faint praise*, they say something about it which sounds quite nice but is not enthusiastic, and shows they do not have a high opinion of it.

"Damned" means condemned. Your lack of authentic, sincere appreciation for the gift of God in your leader condemns you. It means if you are going praise someone or honor someone, don't do it half-heartedly. Don't half clap your hands. "Thou art damned with faint praise."

For instance, one guy might say, "Pastor Smith is an amazing preacher and a phenomenal leader. He can break the word down. He's a preacher's preacher." Then another guy replies, "He's okay." The second person didn't explicitly say anything negative or wrong, yet the faintness of his praise spoke volumes about his opinion of Pastor Smith.

Don't be ashamed to be proud of, and even brag on, your spiritual father. God is not intimidated by the honor you give to the person he sets over your life.

> *And David said to all the congregation, Now bless the LORD your God. And all the congregation blessed the LORD God of their fathers, and bowed down their heads, and worshipped the LORD, and the king.* — ***1 Chronicles 29:20 (KJV)***

The people of Israel literally worshipped God as the Supreme Ruler of the Universe, and they honored David. The people didn't give David any praise or glory that belonged to God. They just honored him as God's representative for being persistent in obeying God's instructions for them. It was like saying, "I thank God for giving us the plan and the strength, but I thank the man of God for being obedient to God."

Because a spiritual parent has given his or her time, energy, and wisdom into ensuring that you succeed in every way imaginable, it is important to show appreciation for your spiritual father or mother by honoring that person, by affixing value to that person, and by making sure they receive whatever it is you have set aside for them, be it money, words of affirmation, time, service, etc.

Honor Is a Lifestyle

> *Honor your father and your mother, so that you may live long in the land the LORD your God is giving you.* — ***Exodus 20:12 (NIV)***

Of all the Ten Commandments, the command to honor your father and mother is the only one with a promise attached to it. Honoring our parents extends the blessings of God in our lives, while dishonoring them cuts those blessings short.

When you honor those who lead you and guide you, by habitually showing them respect and appreciation, your reward is a life full of the greatest possible measure of God's blessing.

It's crucial to remember honoring our parents, whether our earthly parents or our spiritual parents, is not a one-time event, much as God's promise of blessing is not a one-and-done promise. It extends over time. It is a long-term commitment.

Honor requires daily discipline and a commitment to consistently appreciate your spiritual father and those who consistently sow into your life.

Honor is not an event; honor is a lifestyle.

Spiritual Fathers Lead Us Toward Our Destinies

It's never right to be a recipient of your leaders' influence and platform while simultaneously despising their wisdom and correction. Always be a student in the presence of greatness, because when God gives you a real man or woman of God, God will use him or her to speak life into your destiny until things come together.

Spiritual fathers do not just proclaim the Word of God; they also provide spiritual direction and insight for your journey. In the same way the spirit of the Lord began to move upon the prophet Ezekiel and carried him out in the valley of dry bones, God uses spiritual fathers to speak to the dry areas of your life, so you might be able to live, breathe, and move into your God-ordained purpose.

Ezekiel felt God telling him to prophesy to the bones (Ezekiel 37:4), so he did. He began to prophesy until the bones came together and until every joint was connected where they were supposed to connect.

This is a great picture of spiritual fathers. Spiritual fathers are charged with a God-given responsibility to see your destiny and to prophesy and preach until every part of your purpose connects, until you are fully walking in God's plan for your life.

> *From whom the whole body, being fitted and held together by what every joint supplies, according to the proper working of each individual part, causes the growth of the body for the building up of itself in love.* — ***Ephesians 4:16 (NASB)***

Also, think about the process of getting those bones—or rather, our lives—in order. As the bones came together, I'm sure at some point the foot touched the thigh and the thigh touched the spine. But just because they were touching didn't mean that's where those bones were meant to connect.

Sometimes we make the wrong connections, so the man of God has to stand up week after week and continue to preach until bones come together with bones and we start making the right connections. Then we start looking like God intended us to look.

And there are times when we're working on getting our connections right, and then God blesses us. We may not understand why God has blessed us the way He has or why He brought us where He's brought us, but we've been under a prophetic word moving us to the place we are supposed to connect.

God brings us to a church, and the church acts like a spiritual hub. I travel a lot, speaking all over the country. Many times, if I want to fly from one area of the country to another, I have to make a stop in a "hub airport." The hub has more flights to more destinations with shorter travel time.

The place where God plants you is your hub. It's the shortcut to your destiny. In the New Testament, Jerusalem and Antioch were hub cities. The Christians could not go into their ministries until they went to one of these hub cities and were sent out by the Apostles.

You may be at the "hub-airport." You may have a ticket in your hand (predestination). But if you don't make your connecting flight, you will still be stuck in the same place. Some people never arrive at their destination because they come to the hub, but they never connect.

God puts spiritual fathers in our lives, and those fathers are working tirelessly on our behalf, preaching and prophesying.

All of this leads us toward our destinies when we're willing to connect in the right place. When we're willing to change.

Replacing the Ark

> *I will give you shepherds after my own heart, who will lead you with knowledge and understanding.* — ***Jeremiah 3:15 (NIV)***

This is a great verse for spiritual fathers, because it shows that God placed responsibility on the man of God to oversee the spiritual wellbeing of others.[10]

But you really can't stop reading there. I often tell people that you cannot read Jeremiah 3:15 if you don't read the next verse. Jeremiah 3:16 continues: "In those days, when your numbers have increased greatly in the land," declares the Lord, "people will no longer say, 'the ark of the covenant of the Lord.' It will never enter their minds or be remembered; it will not be missed, nor will another one be made" (NIV).

God was taking away His ark so that one day He could give His people what they truly needed—Jesus, the perfect Shepherd. In the meantime, He gave His people human shepherds to guide them in righteousness.

Now, the Ark was where the presence of God was, and it contained three things: Aaron's rod that budded (the miracle), a jar of bread (the manna), and the Ten Commandments (the message). Manna represented the bread for daily life, and the Ten Commandments were the Word of God.[11]

So, God was saying that in the day He gives us shepherds and takes away the ark. The message, the miracle, and the manna we need will be in His shepherds. In place of physical objects that represented the presence of God to His people, He left His children in the care of spiritual fathers. This is why spiritual fathers are so special to God: they represent Him to others (2 Corinthians 5:20).

In 1 Corinthians 4:15, the Scriptures say we may have many instructors, but not many fathers. Many people can teach Sunday school and give you a Bible lesson, but not many people can carry you in their heart like a spiritual father does. Not everyone can preach the Word in a way that speaks to exactly what you've been going through or the challenges you've been facing.

How is it that a pastor can stand up every Sunday and preach to the masses, yet it seems as if they are preaching just to you? This is what a father does. It is a very, very special thing—one we should never take lightly.

We Are Like Children

> *Now I say, That the heir, as long as he is a child, differeth nothing from a servant, though he be lord of all; But is under tutors and governors until the time appointed of the father.* — ***Galatians 4:1–2 (KJV)***

According to this passage, a child heir is really no different from a servant. Even though the child may be lord over a great fortune and people, he lacks all of the skills and knowledge to make him a leader. To fix this, the child heir is placed under tutors and governors until he is ready—until his father appoints him.

Every single one of us is an heir to greatness and giftings. But it is not released until we are mature. We haven't yet been appointed and anointed. We are given the opportunity to grow into what God has for us. He places us under tutors (teachers) and governors (boundaries) until the father sees we are ready to handle more.

We live in an age where a lot of Christians don't like having teachers or boundaries because they think it imposes on the liberty they have in Christ. If the son is not willing to be taught by someone else, how can he teach someone else one day?

I often use the analogy of cement as it relates to boundaries. When cement is being poured, the cement finishers use governors (forms or boards) to cause the cement to harden in a particular shape. If the forms aren't used, the cement hardens into a blob or unwanted shape. If the cement hardens into a cement blob, then the finisher has to use the jackhammer to break up the areas that are undesired.

Many times, God allows the fathers to set boundaries, so sons and daughters can learn personal discipline and not live a life out of control. He doesn't want them to become fixed and unyielding in an undesirable place in their lives.

God wants you to walk in purpose, but you must be willing to submit to a father for guidance and instruction. If not, you'll never receive all God has for you. You will never be better than a child who has an inheritance he can't access.

Don't Provoke Your Sons to Anger

> *And, ye fathers, provoke not your children to wrath: but bring them up in the nurture and admonition of the Lord.*
> ***— Ephesians 6:4 (KJV)***

Some fathers hate to face the fact that everyone we pastor and see birthed into purpose won't be with us forever. Sometimes it's ego and other times it's simply insecurity.

I've seen them pronounce curses on people and tell them they would never prosper if they left their ministry. I've seen them denigrate their sons' character and malign them because they made a decision the father didn't agree with. This ultimately results in sons and daughters walking away without the fathers' blessing, and in many cases, cut off from communication.

We should talk about how to handle separation before we ever separate. Things happen. Life happens. People don't always stay connected. Agree, that if perhaps something were to ever happen in the relationship, you are not going to be at odds with each other. It should be a father's joy to bless their sons when they leave home. The sad thing is there are some churches and ministries who have never been afforded the joy of seeing a son or daughter blessed publicly, because in their eyes, for someone to leave them is simply *wrong*. If you serve a pastor or ministry that has been around a while and no one has ever "left right," this should raise a red flag.

Maybe our problem is not with rebellious sons, but rather with selfish fathers who retard the growth of their adult sons by refusing to allow them to make decisions that accompany adulthood. Some adult decisions are risky. Watching your son make risky decisions is hard, but at that moment you must trust the investment you have made in them. And, be okay if they do miss it or mess up. A father's unconditional love should feel like a "safety net." Fathers don't kick sons for falling, they help them recover and regroup for their next season.

Growing up in my biological father's home, no matter how bad the mistake, at no time did I ever feel like I could not come home.

We treat our spiritual sons like they're our students and mentees, not our "sons." We would never let our natural sons endure some of the things we let our spiritual sons endure.

My son is 21 now, and can physiologically produce children of his own. I just want him to do it in order, and stay connected to his dad. That means, he has to venture out and find his own life. He doesn't have to do it alone because my counsel will be here every step of the way. You may outgrow your father's public success, but you should never outgrow his private counsel.

Don't be an insecure father, provoking your children to anger. Some of them are angry because they are never complimented or celebrated. Our desire to see excellence or produce the right "image" sometimes clouds our judgment, causing us to forget we are in the "people-business." We develop people.

The Abusive Father

One cannot deny the affect abusive fathers have on their families. We see the families who've been victims of abusive fathers, and the unfortunate consequences inflicted on those who cannot defend themselves. We see children, who suffered at the hand of abusive fathers, and the difficulties they face dealing with abandonment, rejection, rage, and self-sabotaging behaviors. Everyday we're bombarded with news reports highlighting dysfunctional family activities, where abusive fathers are at the root. But, what does one do when they encounter an abusive spiritual father in the church? What does one do when an abusive spiritual father unleashes their wrath on a person or people who have embraced the anointed call on their lives?

Dealing with the residue of an abusive father in the home is one thing, but handling an abusive spiritual father in your worship place is truly another. Abusive spiritual fathers are not necessarily identified right away. Initial contact with them is exciting and uplifting. Many of the congregants do not recognize the manipulative, controlling, and divisive characteristics lurking beneath their charismatic, compelling, and captivating mannerisms. As fathers, we are called to lovingly lead, but never to control. However, if sons and daughters remain compliant, loyal, self-sacrificing, and un-confrontational, they are supposedly "safe." But, as soon as they raise questions or queries regarding leadership approaches, personal behaviors, and ministry matters, they are targeted as the enemy, and are ducking the javelins of character assassination and ministry maligning.

Once exposed, abusive spiritual fathers seek to slander, defame, and criticize those who choose to stand for the God in them, rather than their current behaviors. God never intended anyone to serve as a cover for wrong. I have heard of stories where young ministers were actually the front for the devious, illicit, and immoral behavior of their leaders. God never expects you to endorse wrong to prove your loyalty.

Suddenly, the anointing on the sons which was once openly celebrated and acknowledged by the leader is now in error, and they're a demonic force sent to steal, kill, and destroy their sons' lives. Spiritually abusive fathers and mothers revel in public defamations of character and pulpit proclamations cloaked in innuendo and inference, as if those who are their targets are clueless to the direction of their barbs. Support is withdrawn, and backing is inhibited. Even prayers are prayed alluding to their sons' so-called "rebellion" and Jezebel-uprising. They are discredited, disgraced, and shamed because they "came against" the move of God.

As if that were not enough, spiritual abusive fathers will undermine any godly relationships their sons have established within the ministry. Directives designed to isolate their sons and insulate themselves are employed. Those that served with them are threatened with demotion if they remain in the supposed wayward son's company. Many are placed in a position of choosing sides, with scripture used as foundation for the abusive father's "us and them" attacks. They are labeled "blessing blockers," "prodigal sons and daughters," and accused of harboring "questioning spirits." The sons are left shell-shocked and battle fatigued from the viciousness and the veracity of their father's actions. Left spiritually depleted, they're discouraged and severely wounded because of their loyalty to God first, rather than worshipping their abusive spiritual fathers.

It is easy as a leader to get caught up in the attention and loyalty expressed by those who have identified us as their spiritual father. We must be careful. The enemy will use our own personal weaknesses, insecurities, and broken places to shift the focus from God to us. Our charge as "more than a mentor" is to 1) recognize our own areas of needed spiritual development and growth; 2) be intentional about allowing the Holy Ghost to minister to us in those areas; 3) be open to developmental dialogue from those around us; 4) give people permission to leave, celebrating the God who dwells in them; 5) set up guidelines for transition, to include appropriate explanations; and 6) focus on the relationship rather than on the transition.

As much as we don't want to admit it, sometimes God uses the next leader in a person's life to teach them the things that they could not get from you. David was a product of mixed-mentoring. Jesse could teach him how to be a shepherd, but he could not teach him how to be a king. He had to go to the House of Saul.

Don't get mad when people leave you. Remember, three-fourths of the people you lead came from somewhere else. An old man told me something that I will never forget, when I was a young pastor and the first group of people left my church. He said, "Son, get used to people coming and going, because as long as the church is alive, that's two things people are going to do." You cannot take everything personally. The people that God has for you are all coming if you make the resolve to never become bitter.

WORKBOOK

Chapter 1 Questions

Question: What roles do spiritual fathers play in the church and in the lives of their spiritual sons and daughters? What spiritual mentors have you had, and what roles did they play in your life?

Question: What are the chief benefits of having a strong relationship with a spiritual father? Which of these benefits seem(s) most important to you in terms of growing in your relationship with God?

____

____

____

____

Action: Get in the habit of showing your God-given spiritual leader the utmost respect. Make a lifestyle choice to honor your spiritual parents just as fully as God wants you to honor your earthly parents.

Chapter 1 Notes

CHAPTER TWO

The Responsibilities of the Sons and Daughters

The spiritual fathers aren't the only ones with responsibilities and callings. The followers, or sons and daughters, have them too.

In Exodus 28, God raised up spiritual fathers. Verse 1 says: "Have Aaron your brother brought to you from among the Israelites, along with his sons Nadab and Abihu, Eleazar and Ithamar, so they may serve me as priests."

Aaron's sons were Nadab, Abihu, Eleazar, and Ithamar. The meanings of their names typify the five-fold ministry. The name Aaron means "teacher." Nadab means "voluntary gift" (like an evangelist going here and there). Abihu means "he is my father" (like an apostle). Eleazar means "mouth of God" (like a prophet). Ithamar means "island of the palm tree," but was also used to mean "the father of Tamar" (like a pastor).[12] The Palm Tree is rooted and stable. When the hurricane hits the coast of Florida, the palm trees bend all the way over under the assault of torrential rain. When the storm passes, it stands erect again and lends shade to those who come under it for covering. That is what a true pastor and father does.

God wanted these men to be set apart, so He instructed that priestly garments be made for them to give them "dignity and honor" (Exodus 28:2 NIV). By giving them these garments, God was setting them apart. He was identifying them as men of God, as leaders. The garments were also an outward expression of the inner relationship the individual had with God.

> *Aaron and his sons must wear them whenever they enter the tent of meeting or approach the altar to minister in the Holy Place, so that they will not incur guilt and die. —* ***Exodus 28:43 (NIV)***

The sons had to wear Aaron's consecrated garments for seven days:

> *The holy garments for Aaron shall be his sons after him; they shall be anointed in them and ordained in them. The son who succeeds him as priest, who comes into the tent of meeting to minister in the Holy Place, shall wear them seven days. —* ***Exodus 29:29–30 (ESV)***

This passage is about the mantle of the priest. In particular, the mantle of a father of priests. The son who would actually take the place of his father at some point had to wear his father's covering for seven days. Seven in the scripture is always related to "perfection." The sons literally had to be perfected in the mantle, vision, and anointing of their father. It speaks of a transfer. When you make the decision that you are going to stand even as your father has stood and do business on behalf of heaven, the same weight that is on his assignment is now on you and your assignment. You wear it. You wear his mantle.

But there is also something very interesting about the high priest's (or the spiritual father's) garment.

> *Make sacred garments for your brother Aaron to give him dignity and honor. Tell all the skilled workers to whom I have given wisdom in such matters that they are to make garments for Aaron, for his consecration, so he may serve me as priest.* — ***Exodus 28:2–3 (NIV)***

All Levites were priests, but the sons of Aaron were High Priests. We are all priests and kings unto God (Revelations 1:6), but God has always had leaders among leaders.

Each priest made his own garment. The high priests didn't make garments for themselves; instead the "wise, skilled workers" made the garments for them. It takes a congregation to make the covering. How do you weave a covering for your pastor? Every time you support his vision, pray for your pastor, listen to his counsel, encourage his ministry, sow financially to the ministry, worship with ministry, you are "making a garment" for him. You actually cover your leader. *You make the leader a garment.*

There was something different about the high priest's garment. One of the most striking differences was the breastplate. On the chest of the high priest's garment were twelve stones (Exodus 28:17–21), and those stones represented the twelve tribes of Israel.[13]

The man of God literally carried the images of the families of the church on his breast. After Sunday services, when the pastor leaves and he goes home, he doesn't just go home in what you see him clothed in. He goes home in the garment or covering the people covered him with. And the people of God—the people in his congregation—are on his chest and heart.

When he walked before God in His presence, he carried all the people on his heart. The man of God carries you on his heart. When he prays, God doesn't see him in his suit, He sees him praying in that tailor-made garment that the saints covered him with. God sees your image on the man of God and God blesses you wherever you are because you are connected to His servant.

Every day, he carries you on his heart. When he goes to pray, you're with him. You are attached to his covering. When he's thinking about his ministry, you're with him. This is the incredible responsibility of a spiritual father for those God has given him. You are on his mind and heart every single day. And when he is going to God, he can't help but take you with him. When he prays and God responds, God goes into *your* future and starts pouring out blessings and opening doors, because you are attached to his covering. We're blessed, often not because of us, but rather because of who we are connected to.

A Serious Call for a Serious Situation

Jesus takes 12 men, some whom have never even been to Bible school, and He sends them out in His name (Matthew 10:1; Luke 9:1). Remember, apostolic authority is authorized to deputize. When they go out in His name and under his covering, demons are subject to them. The spirit world is afraid of what is being preached and the purpose of the church. The spirit world cringes when pastors and spiritual leaders get on their knees.

If you understand this, then you understand the devil is in trouble.

And you also understand the great responsibility given to spiritual fathers—responsibility to raise up champions and leaders. To bring truth to every single person.

You may have experienced this.

You may have been "tore up from the floor up" until you found a faithful church with a faithful man or woman of God. You may have been backwards as backwards could be. Your family might have been troubled till you came to a faithful church and sat under a faithful leader. You didn't work a job consistently. You didn't follow through with your responsibilities until you came to a faithful church. It was the Word of God that changed you, and the spiritual leaders helped you get there.

Stand by Your Pastor

Your spiritual father has a weighty calling upon his life. He carries the burden of the Word of the Lord (Zechariah 9:1, 12:1; Malachi 1:1). He trains you up to be like Christ. He speaks truth into your life. He shows you love, compassion, and a better way of living.

Fathers bring government (the structure), fear (the reverence), discipline (the correction), and authority (the standard). An example of this happened when I was a little boy. I would be jumping up and down on the bed violently, then I would hear my sister say, "Daddy's home!" My entire demeanor would change because he had established the rule of "no jumping on the bed." I respected his presence, but I knew he also had the right to discipline me if I disobeyed his words. It wasn't that my dad didn't like for me to have fun. It was that he didn't want me putting myself at risk of getting hurt and possibly requiring stitches, all in the name of having fun. It wasn't until I was grown and had children of my own that I realized the weight of the responsibility for the well-being of my family. It made me appreciate my dad even more.

Because they carry these concerns, spiritual fathers need their sons and daughters to stand by them. Relationships exist and thrive because of mutual support, mutual assistance, and mutual compassion. If your father has poured into you, then you should be willing to support him or her when opposition arises.

In John 18, the religious leaders and soldiers came to arrest Jesus, but Peter wasn't having any of it. He drew his sword and cut off a man's ear. Jesus had to calm him down and assure him that what was happening was okay. But what we see from this is, Peter was willing to defend Jesus to the end.

Peter's actions were wrong, but his instinct revealed a willingness to protect the man who had always protected him. In the same way, we must be willing to protect those who protect us. We must fight for those who have fought for us. And we must storm the gates of heaven for those who have stormed heaven for us.

Sure, your pastor can pray for himself, but he has raised up men and women to help him so he isn't doing it all alone. Sure, he can stand up for himself, but if someone is coming against him, I'm sure he would appreciate some support.

As he has been there for you, so you should be there for him. He has helped you. He has shown you the way. He has been there through ups and downs. When and if your spiritual father needs "backup," don't leave him to have to fight for himself, help him! Assist the one who has always assisted you. Most importantly, don't leave his side until the Lord releases you.

There is a storm that will hit the life of every God-anointed leader, and will make him want to change his vocation. I'm reminded again of the story of Noah and his sons. In Genesis 9:20–23, after the ark rested, Noah began to be a farmer, planted a vineyard, and got drunk. After enduring such a terrible storm, the guy who had preached 120 years *changed his vocation* and began to be a farmer.

Noah planted a vineyard and got drunk off the grapes. His son, Ham, saw him drunk and naked in his tent. I submit to you that if he was drunk *in his tent* that the news should have stayed *in his tent*. Ham immediately went out to spread the news. Noah's other sons, Shem and Japheth, took a cloth and placed it over their shoulders, backed up and covered their father.

See the difference in the sons. One son wanted to make sure it was known, while the other two honored their father enough to not try to shame him. I'm not a proponent of cover-up, but I am a proponent of cover*ing*. Shem and Japheth were not so quick to forget how God just used their father, Noah, to save the entire world. So, in his weakness, they walked in backward and dropped the cloth over him.

The Price Your Pastor Pays

It is painful for a church to lose a member. We grieve when we lose a church member. We feel the blow if we lose a good deacon. But what happens when you lose the church's main spiritual leader?

When we look at King David and his relationship with his men, we learn some interesting things. In 2 Samuel 18:3, David was getting ready for battle:

> *But the men said, "You must not go out; if we are forced to flee, they won't care about us. Even if half of us die, they won't care; but you are worth ten thousand of us. It would be better now for you to give us support from the city."* ***— 2 Samuel 18:3 (NIV)***

I want you to consider what comes against your life. If you have a demon or two coming against you every week, think about what the spiritual leader in your life is facing and multiply that attack five hundred times. He carries everyone's burdens. He carries the vision for the church. He has the strategy for the next "win." He has a grace to deal with situations which would have the average man pulling his hair out. He or she is not like just another member. David's men said, "You are worth ten thousand of us." Imagine what he is up against!

Zechariah 13:7 observes, "Strike the shepherd, and the sheep will be scattered..." (NIV). The enemy sends opposition to headship and leadership first. The job of the enemy is to get to all the sons and daughters and get them discombobulated. Satan hits the leader to ensure there is no solidarity among the sheep.

And Luke 22:31 says, "Satan has asked to sift all of you as wheat" (NIV).

Essentially, if the spiritual leader goes down, we all go down.

I don't know about you, but that's something that haunts me. That's a reason to add my pastor to my daily prayer list. That's a reason to pray for his family every time I pray for mine.

Your spiritual father is up against some powerful foes, and he needs your support as much as possible.

Together Until the End

There is a touching story in the Bible of Elijah and Elisha.

> *When the LORD was about to take Elijah up to heaven in a whirlwind, Elijah and Elisha were on their way from Gilgal. Elijah said to Elisha, "Stay here; the LORD has sent me to Bethel." But Elisha said, "As surely as the LORD lives and as you live, I will not leave you." So they went down to Bethel. The company of the prophets at Bethel came out to Elisha and asked, "Do you know that the LORD is going to take your master from you today?"* "Yes, I know," *Elisha replied, "so be quiet." Then Elijah said to him, "Stay here, Elisha; the Lord has sent me to Jericho." And he replied, "As surely as the Lord lives and as you live, I will not leave you." So they went to Jericho. The company of the prophets at Jericho went up to Elisha and asked him, "Do you know that the Lord is going to take your master from you today?" "Yes, I know," he replied, "so be quiet." Then Elijah said to him, "Stay here; the Lord has sent me to the Jordan." And he replied, "As surely as the Lord lives and as you live, I will not leave you." So the two of them walked on. Fifty men from the company of the prophets went and stood at a distance, facing the place where Elijah and Elisha had stopped at the Jordan. Elijah took his cloak, rolled it up and struck the water with it. The water divided to the right and to the left, and the two of them crossed over on dry ground. When they had crossed, Elijah said to Elisha, "Tell me, what can I do for you before I am taken from you?" Let me inherit a double portion of your spirit," Elisha replied. "You have asked a difficult thing," Elijah said, "yet if you see me when I am taken from you, it will be yours—otherwise, it will not." As they were walking along and talking together, suddenly a chariot of fire and horses of fire appeared and separated the two of them, and Elijah went up to heaven in a whirlwind. Elisha saw this and cried out, "My father! My father! The chariots and horsemen of Israel!" And Elisha*

*saw him no more. Then he took hold of his garment and tore it in two. — **2 Kings 2:1–12 (NIV)***

Many in ministry have the *mechanics* of fathering but lack the *dynamics*. Therefore, like Elijah, who had no spiritual father, they become "sons of a single portion." Elisha received a double portion. It was because Elijah was his father. Upon his ascension, he called out, "My Father, My Father..." Notice, he did not say, "My Teacher, My Teacher or My Mentor, My Mentor. He said, "My Father, My Father."

Elijah had trained Elisha up. He had been his spiritual father, teaching him everything he knew. When Elijah died, Elisha went and struck the waters and asked, "Where is the Lord God of Elijah?" He was connected to that man.

And even in Elijah's old age and at Elijah's request, Elisha refused to leave his side. He refused to part from the man who had meant so much to him. And in the end, Elisha got the double portion blessing for which he had asked.

Let's look at Elisha's double portion. Theologians say Elijah the prophet did 16 miracles, but Elisha only did 31 in his life. Then Elisha died. He is dead and in the grave. Some men were burying another corpse when they "spied a band of men." They were in such a hurry to get away, they dumped the dead body they had in the prophet Elisha's open tomb. At the contact with the bones, the man stood up on his feet. That was Elisha's 32nd miracle which gave him double that of his spiritual father. I promise you, God remembers your faithfulness and will give you the double-portion blessing for standing with your leader.

Upon Elisha's deathbed, the King Joash (2 Kings 13:14) referred to Elisha the same way. He said, "My Father, My Father." He had been fathered and he became a father to one whose position was higher than his own. Gehazi, his servant, never became a son in the spirit of God, therefore, he became a bastard in the wrong spirit of greed. This pattern repeats, millenniums later.

The sons of the prophets followed from afar, so when Elijah went up… the mantle didn't fall down on them. Who are you the son of?

There is blessing in standing by your leader, and that blessing trickles down. The leader is blessed, and the followers are blessed. I'm not saying we should support our leaders *only* so we can get a blessing. I'm saying that God recognizes loyalty. He honors it. He sees the heart, and if you stand by your father and support him as much as you can, God will take notice.

The Daddy Wound

I've encountered many authentic, Spirit-led and Spirit-filled leaders who wonder why there isn't an urgent demand placed on the profound anointing they carry. They're tireless in their purpose, efficient in their study, exceptional in their teaching and preaching, and, more importantly, relentless in their pursuit of God and Godly relationships. And yet, many of them wonder why they themselves are not sought after for the wisdom, knowledge, and understanding a seasoned faith journey produces. These individuals want to be more than a mentor. They're recognized and celebrated in Kingdom circles and they've proven their authenticity, transparency, and integrity. Through the leading of the Holy Ghost, they can recognize and identify men and women of God who could truly benefit from their experience and skill. However, they find themselves being rejected and dismissed from those who, perhaps, need them the most for guidance, instruction, and correction. For some reason, these people will not get close to ministry. What is the problem?

The problem is "the daddy wound." We realize the profound affect unhealthy father-child relationships can foster. When a child perceives the father is uninterested, unavailable, uncaring, and unconcerned, a serious breach occurs. Now, the child is left wrestling with rejection, abandonment, and anger issues. They're confused and perplexed. How can the one who seeded me deny me? How can the one I look like be unwilling to look at me? As a result, the child responds out of their wound. They grow up feeling unwanted, unappreciated, and unloved. They seek out other relationships to provide what they would have gotten from their father. They operate in suspicion and distrust. They live with PTSD (Post Traumatic Stress Disorder), seeing an enemy in everyone, responding in full battle mode to protect themselves from feeling neglected again.

Now, make that father a pastor, an elder, a bishop, and so on. Imagine being rejected by the person we look to as our spiritual leader or father. Imagine being told this is our leader, our pastor, the one who is to guide, direct, instruct, form, and inform us. There is excitement about the prospect of a lifelong void being filled. Loyalty is unquestionable. The belief God has placed this individual in our life to push us into our God-given destiny is dominant. Now, consider this. The answer to our spiritual enthusiasm is the same response we received from our natural father. The feelings of abandonment, rejection, and anger surface again. Words like unworthy, incompetent, incapable, useless, and hopeless find their way back into our vocabulary (if they ever left). Not to mention, those feelings, those words are amplified because of the environment—the church.

The same activity exhibited by the unavailable natural father is emphasized. Promises made are never kept. Affirmation is never received. Nothing is ever good enough. Appreciation is non-existing. Lack of interest is evident. Once again, the proverbial child is left wrestling with rejection, abandonment, and anger, not just with the person, but also with God. Oh, and one other point. This encounter has happened multiple times. This "daddy wound" runs deep. It festers and contaminates everything about us. Now, we're not only suffering in the natural, we're grieved in our spirit. This contamination becomes evident and apparent in everything we do. Then we are labeled "renegades" and "Jezebels," because we're perceived as operating outside of a spiritual covering, when in fact, we were under a spiritual smothering.

WORKBOOK

Chapter 2 Questions

Question: How is a spiritual father to be faithful to his spiritual sons and daughters? What specific burdens does a spiritual father carry for his spiritual children?

____

____

____

____

____

____

Question: Have you ever met someone who could not work freely in their present ministry because they had been hurt previously by another leader (Daddy Wound)? How can you help someone like that release the past and receive from their present leader?

____

____

____

____

____

____

____

____

____

____

____

____

____

____

____

____

____

____

Action: Pray for specific guidance from God about how He wants you to support your pastor or other spiritual parent.

Chapter 2 Notes

CHAPTER THREE

Reuniting Father and Son

Not all of us have had the best relationships with our spiritual parents. Some of were left abandoned because of circumstances, leaving them feeling orphaned, while others have flat-out rejected their spiritual parents and gone their own way. Or we've taken the blessing and left everyone who helped us get it behind.

The Prodigal Son

The story of the prodigal son is a powerful example of a son taking what he has gleaned from the father and walking away when you read it through the lens of a spiritual father/spiritual child relationship.

> *Jesus continued: "There was a man who had two sons. The younger one said to his father, 'Father, give me my share of the estate.' So he divided his property between them. Not long after that, the younger son got together all he had, set off for a distant country and there squandered his wealth in wild living. After he had spent everything, there*

was a severe famine in that whole country, and he began to be in need. So he went and hired himself out to a citizen of that country, who sent him to his fields to feed pigs. He longed to fill his stomach with the pods that the pigs were eating, but no one gave him anything. When he came to his senses, he said, 'How many of my father's hired servants have food to spare, and here I am starving to death! I will set out and go back to my father and say to him: Father, I have sinned against heaven and against you. I am no longer worthy to be called your son; make me like one of your hired servants.' So he got up and went to his father. But while he was still a long way off, his father saw him and was filled with compassion for him; he ran to his son, threw his arms around him and kissed him. The son said to him, 'Father, I have sinned against heaven and against you. I am no longer worthy to be called your son.' But the father said to his servants, 'Quick! Bring the best robe and put it on him. Put a ring on his finger and sandals on his feet. Bring the fattened calf and kill it. Let's have a feast and celebrate. For this son of mine was dead and is alive again; he was lost and is found.' So they began to celebrate. Meanwhile, the older son was in the field. When he came near the house, he heard music and dancing. So he called one of the servants and asked him what was going on. 'Your brother has come,' he replied, 'and your father has killed the fattened calf because he has him back safe and sound.' The older brother became angry and refused to go in. So his father went out and pleaded with him. But he answered his father, 'Look! All these years I've been slaving for you and never disobeyed your orders. Yet you never gave me even a young goat so I could celebrate with my friends. But when this son of yours who has squandered your property with prostitutes comes home, you kill the fattened calf for him!' 'My son,' the father said, 'you are always with me, and everything I have is yours. But we had to celebrate and be glad, because this brother of yours was dead and is alive again; he was lost and is found.'" ***— Luke 15:11–32 (NIV)***

The prodigal son received a blessing, and what did he do with it? He took it and left. He thought he could do better on his own. He thought he didn't need his father's guidance any longer. But he ended up wasting his blessing. He wasted it in "wild living." *Wild living* is unorthodox behavior. He wasted what he was.

He goes to a *distant country.* This is the place that doesn't even believe all you have been taught by your ministry father. Then, he connects with the *citizens of that country.* You have to be careful when you connect with those who don't ascribe to your training. These people offered him a job *feeding pigs* for the slaughter. This kosher Jewish guy has no business with pork, but when you join yourself to people who have not been given the training and discipline that you have, they will make you do things you thought you never would do. The prodigal son gets so hungry, and *no man gave him food to eat.* When you have been ordained to be fed in a place and you get out of that place, you will experience your own personal famine and hunger.

The son wasn't in a place he was ordained to be. He was with people who were a terrible influence. He was doing things outside of what he knew was right.

He needed to come home. He needed to ask forgiveness and get back under the guidance of his father in order to turn his life around and reclaim his inheritance.

If this is you, it's time to go home.

The Orphan

David asked, "Is there anyone still left of the house of Saul to whom I can show kindness for Jonathan's sake?" Now there was a servant of Saul's household named Ziba. They summoned him to appear before David, and the king said to him, "Are you Ziba?" "At your service," he replied. The king asked, "Is there no one still alive from the house of Saul to whom I can show God's kindness?" Ziba answered the king, "There is still a son of Jonathan; he is lame in both feet." "Where is he?" the king asked. Ziba answered, "He is at the house of Makir son of Ammiel in Lo Debar." So King David had him brought from Lo Debar, from the house of Makir son of Ammiel. When Mephibosheth son of Jonathan, the son of Saul, came to David, he bowed down to pay him honor. David said, "Mephibosheth!" "At your service," he replied. "Don't be afraid," David said to him, "for I will surely show you kindness for the sake of your father Jonathan. I will restore to you all the land that belonged to your grandfather Saul, and you will always eat at my table." Mephibosheth bowed down and said, "What is your servant, that you should notice a dead dog like me?" Then the king summoned Ziba, Saul's steward, and said to him, "I have given your master's grandson everything that belonged to Saul and his family. You and your sons and your servants are to farm the land for him and bring in the crops, so that your master's grandson may be provided for. And Mephibosheth, grandson of your master, will always eat at my table." (Now Ziba had fifteen sons and twenty servants.) Then Ziba said to the king, "Your servant will do whatever my lord the king commands his servant to do." So Mephibosheth ate at David's table like one of the king's sons. ***— 2 Samuel 9:1–11***

In this particular story, David is remembering the covenant he has with his good friend Jonathan. Jonathan was David's brother-in-law who had died in a battle with his father Saul. When both Saul and Jonathan die, it leaves David's covenant-friend's son orphaned. He has no family.

The Bible says Mephibosheth has been cared for by his nurse. In 2 Samuel 4:4, the news of Saul and Jonathan's death comes from Jezreel, and Mephibosheth's nurse, trying to save him, picks him up in a hurry but drops him and causes him to become disabled. Mephibosheth is both disabled and orphaned, but king David is so concerned about his dear friend's house that he looks to show kindness to any of Jonathan's descendants.

There are situations that leave sons and daughters feeling orphaned, such as the death of a pastor, the sudden dismissal of a pastor, or the cold-shoulder of a pastor. In moments like these, it's easy for the sons and daughters to feel disowned or abandoned. These are sons and daughters of leaders that we are in covenant with who now need to feel they matter and that everything their spiritual father had promised them is still part of their inheritance.

In many cases, there are those who, like Mephibosheth's nurse, are assigned to care for someone in the absence of their father, but who are simply not capable of carrying their weight. 2 Samuel 4:4 says he was five years old when he was dropped by his nurse. Two things can be concluded from this. First of all, he was not the size of a toddler. He was a big boy. Secondly, for the fall to maim a five-year-old boy, it must have been a pretty nasty fall. The job of caring for orphaned sons and daughters is often relegated to nurses (committees, other sons, or institutions). Sometimes when sons and daughters find themselves orphaned by their spiritual father, it takes another spiritual father who was in covenant with their leader to seek them out, as David did Mephibosheth, to bring the healing that the house needs. David didn't look for him because he needed another son. He sought to bless Mephibosheth because of his relationship with his father. David literally became an adoptive father. He blessed him as his own father would have done. He sat him at the table with no requirement on his part but to receive the love being given. Where are the adoptive fathers who seek to heal the orphaned sons? That's what real fathers do, and they do it without ulterior motives.

Get Under the Shadow

> *The apostles performed many signs and wonders among the people. And all the believers used to meet together in Solomon's Colonnade. No one else dared join them, even though they were highly regarded by the people. Nevertheless, more and more men and women believed in the LORD and were added to their number. As a result, people brought the sick into the streets and laid them on beds and mats so that at least Peter's shadow might fall on some of them as he passed by. Crowds gathered also from the towns around Jerusalem, bringing their sick and those tormented by impure spirits, and all of them were healed.*
> ***— Acts 5:12–16 (NIV)***

Peter's shadow was so powerful people were healed simply by being in its path! Leaders should want their influence to be so those who encounter them will know this person has been with Jesus.

What is a shadow? A shadow happens when the rays of the sun reflect on an object and then the object casts the image of itself. This cannot take place without a greater light. The glory is the light of that City, greater than the sun.

> *The city does not need the sun or the moon to shine on it, for the glory of God gives it light, and the Lamb is its lamp. —* ***Revelations 21:23 (NIV)***

Only 50 days after his denial of Jesus, Peter has an anointed shadow. He's only been saved three and a half years. He's only been filled with the Holy Ghost for two short months, but the Spirit of God gives this power in his shadow.

The light shines directly on him so everyone who comes in contact with him will be just like if they touched the hem of Jesus' garments.

Peter cast a shadow of healing and blessing, but the House of God casts a shadow of protection.

> *And the Lord will create upon every dwelling place of mount Zion, and upon her assemblies, a cloud and smoke by day, and the shining of a flaming fire by night: for upon all the glory shall be a defense. And there shall be a tabernacle for a shadow in the daytime from the heat, and for a place of refuge, and for a covert from storm and from rain. —* ***Isaiah 4:5–6 (KJV)***

The tabernacle, or the House of God, will be a shadow in the daytime from the heat (the fiery trials of life).

You may no longer be walking in darkness. You may no longer be in the world. You may have already made a commitment to God and come under the shadow of the man of God, but you need the shadow of the Tabernacle. The church, the *ecclesia*, provides a breeze of shelter from the scorching problems life hurls at us. All scripture is given by inspiration of God. God doesn't waste words. You need to get up under the Shadow.

Is it time for you to get back under the shadow of the one God has placed in your life? Is it time for you to turn back to God and to renew your relationship with your heavenly Father and your spiritual father? Is it time for you to get under the shadow of, and connect with, your local church?

Or perhaps it's time for you to take your participation to the next level.

Bring Me My Coat

In 2 Timothy 4:13, Paul instructed Timothy to bring him his cloak or coat. It was cold, and Paul needed someone to cover him with a garment. And in verse 16, he told Timothy, "No man stood with me, but all men forsook me" (KJV).

Many times, when the man of God gets to the height of his ministry, he looks around and can't find his sons. He wonders, where are those who he poured into and birthed into their ministry?

He is saying, "I need to reap where I have sown. I need them to bring back what I have sowed to them." Your leaders sow their spiritual things; you sow your natural things (1 Corinthians 9:11). It is not enough to say, "I honor you," with your lips. You have to give your money! Your money is seed, and your leaders' life is soil. When you put your seed in your father's life, you will reap a harvest both naturally and spiritually.

Your *move* of God is connected to your *man* of God. Your *promotion* is connected to your *prophet.*

> *The best of all the firstfruits and of all your special gifts will belong to the priests. You are to give them the first portion of your ground meal so that a blessing may rest on your household.* — ***Ezekiel 44:30 (NIV)***

In the Old Testament, the children of Israel were commanded to take care of the priest (the man of God) first, so a blessing would remain on their family.

> *For where your treasure is, there will his heart be also.* — ***Matthew 6:21 (KJV)***

As Paul needed Timothy to bring him his coat, every spiritual father has a need for his sons and daughters to come back and bring them honor. Paul most likely left his coat with Timothy in a time that he needed warmth. Paul was saying, "If I have been covering for you in the early stages of your ministry, now that I am older, I need you to cover me. I need the same help I gave to you."

Perhaps you've been benefitting under the guidance of a spiritual father. Perhaps there is someone who has poured into you, someone who has prayed for you, mentored you, helped you. Perhaps that person has helped you to become who you are today.

But perhaps you haven't fully appreciated or thanked that person.

Now is the time.

Now is the time to thank pastors for loving us when we were unlovable. Now is the time to thank them for investing in our children, for teaching our kids Scripture and songs.

Now is the time to thank your pastor for the sermons that made you uncomfortable because they spoke truth into your life.

Now is the time to tithe to your church, to support with your finances the people who have done so much for you and for your community.

Now is the time to step up. To acknowledge all they have taught and trained and to take on more responsibility. Now is the time to be more than a body in a seat on Sunday morning. Now is the time to participate in the ministry and take your commitment to the next level.

Thank your pastors. Honor them. Love them.

I don't know about you, but I'd be lost right now if the church hadn't saved me. My pastor listened. He poured into me. And then the Lord called me.

Is the Lord calling you? Does He have a promise that He wants to fulfill through you?

Open up. He will see you through, whether you seek to strengthen your current relationship with your spiritual father, rekindle an abandoned relationship, or take on some spiritual children of your own, God's got you.

And He's just getting started.

The Final Word

By now I am hoping you've been reminded of past experiences and present circumstances needing your attention. I am hoping you've been reminded of those who operated as more than a mentor in your life, or those opportunities where you chose to be more than a preacher or instructor in someone else's ministry journey. Perhaps you've recognized some relationships needing your attention, some individuals you must honor properly, realized some behaviors you need to change, or even determined it's time to shift from your current place of ministry and connect with those individuals who have been or will be operating in the capacity of more than a mentor for you.

For those of us who have accepted the call of being more than a mentor, we know there are many destiny seekers hungry for spiritual impartation and willing to listen to honest feedback, positive reinforcement, and dynamic spiritual instruction. We commit to love God's people. We also recognize there are those who have been wounded and discarded waiting to hear the same words from us Jesus spoke to Lazarus (John 11:41–44). There are many who need to hear us say, "Come out of the dead situation you are in." "Come out of the hurt and pain you have experienced in ministry." "Come out of the dry, desert place that has drained and decimated you." And, once they are out, the compassion of God gives us the capacity to tell others, "Loose them and let them go."

No spiritual father is perfect or beyond making mistakes. Most of us have learned, as Jesus learned, through the things we have gone through. Our mistakes and our challenges have been lessons to pass on to future generations.

> *Although He was a Son, He learned obedience from the things which He suffered.* — ***Hebrews 5:8 (NASB)***

Trials will make you question whether or not you're going in the right direction. Know that nothing comes into your life as a surprise to God! He uses our trials to give us a testimony. You have to have a testimony. David met Goliath with a testimony. My spiritual father used to always define a testimony as "an undeniable experience with God in the past which will sustain you through any present difficulty." Your wisdom and experience with God are necessary for those you will lead. The greater the responsibility, the greater the revelation. You don't need a burning bush if you're not going to do anything monumental. We have a tendency to change our testimony when we face trials, but when you have had an undeniable experience with God, you can say, "I know what God showed me and I won't change my mind."

The Kingdom of God is under attack and we need all anointed vessels to war for our prophetic purpose. No one can be cast aside. No one can be left behind. No one can be pushed to the back. No one can be deemed "not valuable." One of my spiritual sons uses the term

AHOD, which means "All Hands On Deck." The enemy has declared war on the church.

Impartation will require the investment of time. Elisha stayed in the presence of Elijah. Ruth remained loyal to Naomi. David sought the counsel of Samuel. You are not their father or mentor if there is no communication.

The enemy has sought to sabotage Godly relationships, assassinate divine connections, and terminate the influences of fathers to their sons. We can no longer be just mentor, just pastor, just preach, or just teach. We must be more than mentor, providing a spiritual legacy to sons and daughters. We must prepare others to receive our mantles of grace, of faithfulness, of effective preaching, of fervent prayer, of intensive stewardship, of New Testament Power, and of intentional focus, to ensure the kingdoms of this world fall to the Kingdom of our God. We are called to help people find where they fit, to place them, and to train them. Israel could not reach their destiny *until* God raised up Moses. We are needed. We are required. We are called to be "more than a mentor."

WORKBOOK

Chapter 3 Questions

Question: When have you distanced yourself from a spiritual father or turned your back on his guidance? What were the consequences?

____

____

____

____

____

____

____

____

____

____

____

____

Question: When in your life have you become alienated from a spiritual father? What were (or are) specific steps to restoring your relationship? What blessings may follow from being a faithful spiritual child?

____

Action: Make a specific, intentional gesture to thank your spiritual father for his guidance. And thank your heavenly Father daily in prayer for your spiritual father!

Chapter 3 Notes

REFERENCES

Notes

1. Stone, Howard W. and James O. Duke. *How to Think Theologically* (3rd ed.). Minneapolis, MN: Fortress Press, 2013.
2. Warnock, George. "Ingredients of the Holy Oil." *Crowned with Oil* (Ch. 5), 2017. http://www.georgewarnock.com/crowned5.html.
3. Gershtein, Sergery and Anna Gershtein. "Hin Conversion Chart." *Convert-me.com.* https://www.convert-me.com/en/convert/history_volume/biblhin.html?u=biblhin&v=1.
4. James, Cynthia. *Anointing: The Gift, the Grace, the Power*. Dallas, TX: Dexterity Publishing, 2015.
5. Borders, Randy. *The Adjutant's Guide to Etiquette.* Shelby, NC: Harvesters Publishing, 2015.
6. "The Circumcision Ceremony: The Brit Milah (Bris) Step by Step." *Chabad.org*. Chabad-Lubavitch Media Center. http://www.chabad.org/

library/article_cdo/aid/1472861/jewish/The-Circumcision-Ceremony.htm.

7. "Honor To Whom Honor?" *What Does the Bible Say?* Faith Independent Baptist Church, 2008. http://www.holybiblesays.org/articles.php?ID=384.
8. "Strong's G5091 – timaō." *Strong's Exhaustive Concordance.* In *Blue Letter Bible.* https://www.blueletterbible.org/lang/lexicon/lexicon.cfm?Strongs=G5091&t=NIV.
9. Pope, Alexander. *The Epistle to Dr. Arbuthnot.* 1735.
10. Guzik, David. "Study Guide for Jeremiah 3 by David Guzik." 2014. In *Blue Letter Bible.* https://www.blueletterbible.org/Comm/guzik_david/StudyGuide2017-Jer/Jer-3.cfm?a=748016.
11. Slick, Matt. "What Was Inside the Ark of the Covenant?" *Christian Apologetics and Research Ministry.* https://carm.org/what-was-inside-the-ark-covenant.
12. "The Biblical Era." *Hebrew Names.* 2016. http://hebrewname.org/period/the-biblical-era.
13. Jastrow, Morris, Jr., Ira Maurice Price, and Louis Ginzberg. "Breastplate of the High Priest." *Jewish Encyclopedia.* 2002. http://www.jewishencyclopedia.com/articles/3668-breastplate-of-the-high-priest.

About the Author

Bishop Randy Borders, an anointed preacher of our time, communicates the gospel message with unmistakable clarity. His ministry challenges believers to flow in God's Divine Order.

He is a graduate of The University of North Carolina at Greensboro.

In 1990, Bishop Borders founded Word of Life Fellowship Church. The church name was officially changed to Faith Harvest Church in March of 1999.

Bishop Borders currently serves as senior pastor of Faith Harvest Church, in Shelby, NC.

Faith Harvest Church has evolved into a multiracial, multifaceted ministry, which include many ministries of edification and outreach. Bishop Borders is also Founder and Presiding Prelate of Harvest Ministries International, Inc., a network of local churches with primary apostolic vision of church planting and strengthening. Since his consecration, Bishop Borders has become part of the Joint College of African-American Pentecostal Bishops Congress.

In June of 2002, Bishop Borders founded Christ Harvest Church in Charlotte, NC. He also founded Covenant Harvest Church in Greer, SC, in November of 2009.

Bishop Borders met the former Norma Lee while attending UNCG. The two were married in June 1994 and have two lovely children—Efrim and Hope.

A published author of the critically acclaimed books *Stay Focused* and *The Adjutant's Guide to Etiquette,* and his latest book, *More than a Mentor*. Bishop Borders travels extensively throughout the United States and abroad as a lecturer, conference speaker, revivalist, and seminar speaker.

The ministry of Bishop Borders is bold, energetic, and dynamic, equipping the saints to lock into their pastor's vision and fulfill their destiny. Many who have experienced his ministry have this testimony: Bishop Borders is definitely a pastor's friend.

About Sermon To Book

SermonToBook.com began with a simple belief: that sermons should be touching lives, *not* collecting dust. That's why we turn sermons into high-quality books that are accessible to people all over the globe.

Turning your sermon series into a book exposes more people to God's Word, better equips you for counseling, accelerates future sermon prep, adds credibility to your ministry, and even helps make ends meet during tight times.

John 21:25 tells us that the world itself couldn't contain the books that would be written about the work of Jesus Christ. Our mission is to try anyway. Because in heaven, there will no longer be a need for sermons or books. Our time is now.

If God so leads you, we'd love to work with you on your sermon or sermon series.

Visit www.sermontobook.com to learn more.

Made in the USA
Columbia, SC
12 April 2018